❖

MEDIEVAL ABBEYS AND CHURCHES OF FIFE

❖

A HERITAGE GUIDE

❖ PREFACE

This guide has been produced as part of a series covering the heritage of Fife. In 1989 Fife Regional Council published 'Fife's Early Archaeological Heritage - A Guide' as the first in the Series. The series, covering a wide range of subjects related to the rich natural and historic environment, will be of interest to both residents and visitors to the region. In 1993 the Regional Council published the second, 'Castles of Fife: A Heritage Guide'.

This Guide to the Abbeys and Churches of Fife is the third book to be produced, and follows a similar format. The first part gives a general introduction which outlines ecclesiastical development in Fife and its importance within society. The second part features some of the best examples arranged in chronological order. Each of the sites is marked on the location plan and an Ordnance Survey Grid Reference (Landranger Series) is given at the end of each entry. Details of how to get there and where to park are also given.

Many of the churches are open to the public but some are within private land and can only be viewed from a distance. Many of these historic buildings are still used for public worship, and further details can be sought from the relevant authorities. For those buildings on private land, permission should first be obtained from the landowner. Some structures are particularly ruinous and the greatest care should be taken when entering. With these words of warning, it is hoped that this Guide will be of help in exploring Fife's rich historic environment. Always remember to be careful and follow the country code.

More detailed publications may be available, particularly from properties in the care of the National Trust for Scotland and Historic Scotland. For further information please see the addresses at the end of this guide.

Access information given was correct for the 1994 season. Visitors are advised to check opening times before making a visit.

St Monans Church

❖
ACKNOWLEDGEMENTS

his guide was written by Richard Fawcett who has studied the architecture of medieval Scotland for many years. Dr Fawcett lives in Kirkcaldy and works as a Principal Inspector of Ancient Monuments with Historic Scotland.

Dr Richard Fawcett

This booklet was edited and compiled by Sarah Govan and Peter Yeoman, and designed by the Graphics section in the Department of Economic Development and Planning.

Fife Regional Council is pleased to acknowledge financial support from the European Regional Development Fund to assist with the publication of the Heritage Series.

Fife Regional Council wishes to thank the following for their kind permission to reproduce their photographs and prints.

Crown Copyright: Historic Scotland for

Black & white photographs of St Andrews Sarcophagus, Leuchars Parish Church, St Rule's Church, Dunfermline Abbey, Aberdour Church, St Andrews Cathedral, Church of the Dominicans, St Andrews

Colour photographs of Leuchars Parish Church, St Andrews Cathedral, Dunfermline Abbey, Inchcolm Abbey, Aberdour Parish Church

Plans of The Churches of St Mary Kirkheugh and St Rule, St Andrews, Dunfermline Abbey, Markinch Parish Church, Leuchars Parish Church, Aberdour Parish Church, Lindores Abbey, Culross Abbey, Balmerino Abbey, Crail Collegiate Church, Carnock Parish Church, Abdie Parish Church, Inverkeithing Friary, St Monans Parish Church, Inchcolm Abbey, St Salvator's Church, St Andrews, Dysart Parish Church, Burntisland Parish Church, Dairsie Parish Church and St Bridget's Church, Dalgety.

Crown Copyright: Royal Commission for the Ancient and Historical Monuments of Scotland for Black & white photographs of St Mary's Kirkheugh, St Rule's Church, Leuchars Parish Church (detail), Inchcolm Abbey, Holy Trinity (1908), St Salvator's College , Bishop Kennedy's Tomb, St Serfs Parish Church, Dysart, Dairsie Parish Church, Leuchars Parish Church

Etchings of St Andrews Cathedral, Incholm Abbey (interior), St Monans Parish Church

Plans for Kirkcaldy Parish Church, St Rule's Church, St Andrews, Holy Trinity Church, St Andrews and St Leonard's College, St Andrews and St Andrews Cathedral.

Colin Wishart for black & white photographs of Markinch Parish Church, Crail Parish Church, Inverkeithing Friary, St Monans Parish Church, St Columba's, Burntisland, Holy Trinity, St Andrews, St Leonard's College and Old Parish Church, Kirkcaldy

ife was an area of outstanding importance for the medieval church. By the mid-ninth century Kinrimund (or Kilrimont - which became St Andrews) was the administrative centre of the Scottish church. Its bishops were to take precedence over all others, eventually being made archbishops in 1472, and the cathedral they built for themselves was the largest church ever raised in Scotland. But Fife has other claims to pre-eminence besides St Andrews. The first Scottish community of monks organised on the Benedictine pattern that had become normal in the rest of Europe was founded at Dunfermline, when St Margaret brought monks from Canterbury in about 1070 to serve in her new church. That community was to gain added importance when its church became the most important burial place of Scotland's royal family, as well as the shrine of St Margaret herself.

To meet the spiritual needs of the layfolk there were probably about fifty six parishes. Most of these were in the deaneries of Fife and Fothrif, within the diocese of St Andrews, though about ten of Fife's parishes were within outlying pockets of the dioceses of Dunkeld and Dunblane. There were also numerous chapels, some of which served the more remote parts of parishes, while others were built to commemorate particular saints or to meet the spiritual needs of the great land-holders and their households. In Fife there were as many as fourteen religious houses of various orders of monks, canons, friars and nuns, and possibly one community of Knights Templars. There were seven or eight collegiate churches and about ten hospitals, all of which would have had chapels attached. It is also worth remembering that the earliest of Scotland's collegiate churches was that of St Mary Kirkheugh in St Andrews.

Such statistics leave little doubt that the church must have played a very important part in the lives of the medieval people of Fife. Few of the early churches are still complete although a large number survive as ruins From them we can witness the full architectural range of the medieval church in Scotland better than in any other region. Fife also has the most complete set of domestic buildings of any religious house in Scotland, in the enchanting island abbey of Inchcolm.

When looking at the history of the church in Fife, we have to start with some of the many legends associated with the early church. It is said that relics of St Andrew reached what was to become the city of St Andrews as early as the fourth century. St Rule (or Regulus) was apparently cast ashore there after he had absconded from Patras with the saint's relics, as part of his effort to prevent the emperor taking them to Constantinople. Only a little less unlikely is the legend which says that St Serf headed a community at Culross in the sixth century, where St Kentigern (or Mungo) grew up before moving on to Glasgow. Such legends may have some basis in folk memories of early Christian leaders in this part of Pictland, and the faith must certainly have been well-established here by the later seventh century. The considerable numbers of early cross slabs at places like Largo, Abercrombie (near Anstruther) and Crail, or the cross shafts at Culross, for example, confirm that Christianity had already taken firm root in Fife during the eighth, ninth and tenth centuries.

The clearest picture of Christian life that emerges around this time is at St Andrews. If any relics of that saint did find their way there, they could have arrived with St Acca, an eighth century bishop of Hexham in Northumbria. He had been forced to take refuge in Pictland in 732 and it is conceivable that he brought with him some of the relics that his predecessor at Hexham, St Wilfrid, had acquired in Rome. We know that an important community existed at Kinrimund in the eighth century, perhaps having been founded by one of the two Pictish kings named Angus. By the end of the century the community was in such a thriving condition that it could produce one of the masterpieces of

European church art of this period, the St Andrews sarcophagus. This magnificent work leaves no doubt that the community was in contact with the leading artistic centres of the day.

St Andrews became the administrative centre of the Scottish church in the ninth century. By the late eleventh century, however, there are signs that the church in Scotland was no longer in such a healthy state. Elsewhere in Europe, however, the church was in the throes of a great period of renewal. The lead was being taken by the great monasteries which followed a way of life established by St Benedict for his abbey at Monte Cassino in southern Italy some time after 525. When St Margaret came to Scotland and married Malcolm III, in about 1070, she cannot have viewed the church here with particular enthusiasm. In introducing Benedictine monks to Dunfermline, she was probably trying to show her adopted country what was being done elsewhere in Europe. She also encouraged existing institutions; to help bring pilgrims to St Andrews, she fostered a ferry across the Forth which came to be known as the Queen's Ferry.

Two of Margaret's sons did most to bring the church into conformity with the rest of Europe, where many new religious orders were emerging through the process of renewal. Alexander I (1107-24) installed a reforming bishop at St Andrews in 1123 and eventually overcame the opposition of the existing clergy to introduce Augustinian canons - of which he himself was one - as the main clergy there. Alexander's youngest brother, David I (1124-53) instigated the greatest period of church and monastery building ever seen in Scotland, funded by individual benefactors as well as the crown.. He re-established Dunfermline as a major Benedictine abbey, and brought Benedictines from Reading to the Isle of May in the Firth of Forth. He also introduced Augustinian canons to Inchcolm in fulfilment of the wishes of Alexander I.

Having lived for many years in England, David was aware of other European religious orders emerging during the first half of the twelfth century. Although he personally did not introduce any into Fife he established houses elsewhere in Scotland, from where they eventually colonised Fife. As a consequence there were soon to be Tironensian monks at Lindores and Cistercians at Balmerino and Culross.

St Andrews Sarcophagus

David I also encouraged the founding of parishes to meet the needs of the ordinary people of his kingdom. Many of Fife's parishes were created during his reign, often covering the same area as the landlord's estate. It is likely that Leuchars, one of the finest twelfth-century parish churches anywhere in Scotland, was built at this time. Many of Fife's parish churches were in existence by the 1240s when the energetic Bishop David de Bernham saw it as his particular task to carry out dedications ensuring that they were suitable places for worship. Unfortunately this has introduced an element of confusion as many modern parishes regard these dedications as an indication of when their church was first built, though this is seldom the case.

The basic requirement for a parish church was a chancel and a nave, and there was usually a divided financial responsibility for the two parts: the rector paid for the building and upkeep of the chancel and the layfolk for that of the nave. However, most Scottish parish churches were granted to some monastery or cathedral and, when the rector was some other religious organisation, less interest was probably shown in the fabric of the chancel. This may have been one of the reasons why, from the end of the twelfth century, many Scottish churches came to be built as rectangular structures. For example, at Carnock there was no structural differentiation between the chancel and nave, though there would always have been a screen of some form to separate them.

In thinking about the medieval church it is important to remember that it was not an unchanging institution. In fact, just as the early church had seen a decline in fervour, so there were later periods of decline and renewal. From the thirteenth century onwards this is best seen in the emergence of the orders of friars who tried to live a life modelled on that of the apostles, by

Leuchars Church

8

ministering to the people and living from their offerings. Fife had Dominican friaries at Cupar, St Monans and St Andrews, and Franciscan friaries at Inverkeithing and St Andrews. But even the orders of friars went through periods of decline and renewal, and the two friaries at St Andrews represented late medieval phases of a revival of stricter standards.

Another aspect of medieval ecclesiastical life that is well-represented in Fife is the collegiate church, served by groups of priests living a corporate life. The earliest of these to be established anywhere in Scotland was in the church of St Mary Kirkheugh at St Andrews, founded in about 1250. There the successors of the earlier clergy who had served the main church were formed into what was almost a rival cathedral chapter. But most colleges were of late medieval date, and had as their chief function the offering of prayers for the souls of their founders. The majority of colleges had additional functions, and could also be set up in the major burgh churches, which often had large numbers of clergy serving their various altars. This was the case at Crail in 1517.

Fife played a leading part in the Reformation of 1560 which rejected the authority of the Pope and abolished the mass as the chief form of worship. Discontent had been developing in Fife over many years against the abuses that had emerged within parts of the church. A new focus for the would-be reformers was provided in 1546 with the execution of the reformer George Wishart by Cardinal David Beaton, followed not long afterwards by the Cardinal's own murder within his castle at St Andrews. After John Knox allied himself with those protestants besieged within the castle following the murder, he preached the first of his great sermons in the parish church at St Andrews in 1547. A later sermon by him in the same place, in 1559, led to the 'cleansing' of all the churches in St Andrews of the furnishings associated with the old forms of worship. Many statues, paintings and relics were destroyed, and structural damage was inevitably caused at the same time.

Yet it must not be assumed that the Church of Scotland, as we now know it, emerged ready-made immediately after 1560. On the whole the Scottish Reformation was a relatively gentle process. Most of the old clergy were able to retain the greater part of their income and property, even if they did not wish to serve the new church. Many monks and canons similarly chose to remain within their monasteries, even if they were not allowed to worship openly as before. The presbyterian system only developed after Andrew Melville became a dominant figure from the later 1570s. Indeed, for many years the system of church government fluctuated considerably, with bishops only being finally abolished from the established church in 1689.

The reformed church was so poor at first that it could afford to undertake very little new building, and had to adapt the existing stock of churches for its needs. However, two Fife churches are among the finest illustrations in Scotland of the types of structure that might have been built if more money had been available. At Burntisland a church was started in about 1592, when presbyterianism was in the ascendant, and is essentially an elegant centralised preaching hall. When bishops were again dominant Archbishop John Spottiswood built Dairsie church in 1621, which was intended as a model for a return to more traditional forms of worship. So, even after the Reformation, Fife still illustrates better than most areas the types of buildings that were erected to meet the changing needs of the Scottish church.

Much probably still remains to be discovered about our earlier church buildings, since many post-Reformation churches occupy the sites of their medieval predecessors, and unsuspected medieval work may yet be identified in the course of repairs.

Before moving on to look at the individual abbeys and churches, it may be advisable to offer a brief explanation of some of the more unusual terms that will be used in describing the medieval church and its buildings.

❖
GLOSSARY

abbey - a monastery headed by an abbot.

aisle - this can be either a side space running parallel to the main spaces of a church and separated from it by arches, or a structure projecting laterally from a church to contain additional altars or pews.

altar - a table, usually of stone, at which mass was celebrated. As well as the high altar, most churches would have had a number of lesser altars.

apse - a semi-circular or polygonal termination to the east end or (more uncommonly) flank of a church, which usually contained a principal altar.

arcades - a series of arches, usually carried on columns or piers, separating aisles from main spaces.

arcading - a series of arches, forming part of the decorative treatment of a wall surface.

bays - the divisions down the length of a building that are marked by the piers of an arcade and/or by external buttresses.

bishop - one of the chief officers of the church, responsible for administering an area known as a diocese.

buttress - a vertical thickening of the wall projecting at right angles to the main wall face, and designed to give it additional strength.

canons, regular - clergy living a form of monastic life, although they were not monks in the strictest sense of the word.

canons, secular - clergy serving a cathedral or collegiate church.

cathedral - the church of a bishop, usually the most important church in his diocese.

chancel - the part of the church in which the high altar was set and in which the clergy officiated; in larger churches it might be divided into a presbytery for the former function and a choir for the latter.

chapel - this could be an area within a church where an altar was situated, an off-shoot from a church built to house an altar, or a free-standing church that was usually subservient to a parish church.

chapter house - the meeting room of the canons or monks of a major ecclesiastical establishment.

choir - the area where the clergy sat during services, but sometimes applied to the whole eastern arm of the church, including the area occupied by the high altar.

choir stalls - the timber seats occupied by the clergy within the choir, sometimes with canopies rising above them.

clearstorey - an upper tier of windows rising above the aisles flanking the main spaces of a church.

cloister - the open space around which the domestic buildings of a monastery or friary were grouped, against the flank of the church. It was a square with covered walkways around its perimeter.

college - a group of clergy serving a church area and following a particular set of rules.

columns - cylindrical piers supporting the arches of an arcade.

commendator - an administrative head of a monastery who was not a member of the order represented at that monastery, usually a royal appointee.

Culdees - 'servants of god', clergy within the early church who were originally distinguished by the particular fervour of their religious life; the description was later applied far more loosely.

daughter house - a new monastery founded as an off-shoot of an existing one, and initially staffed by a contingent of their monks

diocese - the area administered by a bishop, and usually divided into archdeaconries, deaneries and parishes.

dormitory - the sleeping hall in a monastery, which usually ran along the first floor of the east range.

friars - members of the Dominican, Franciscan and Carmelite orders, who originally lived by the offerings of those to whom they preached.

friary - a community of friars.

hermit - a holy man living a solitary existence.

Knights Templar - An order of knights who took vows to lead a monastic life. Their chief original function was to protect pilgrims en route to the shrines in the Holy land.

lay brethren - several orders, especially the Cistercians, had illiterate brethren who carried out much of the physical labour of the communities and their estates.

loft - in medieval churches this might be a platform on top of the screen between the nave and chancel. In post-Reformation churches it could either be a timber gallery within the main spaces of the church, or the upper level of a family aisle built against a church.

mass - the celebration of the eucharist, the principal service of the medieval church.

monks - communities of men following vows of poverty, chastity and obedience within a monastery.

nave - the part of the church to the west of the chancel or choir, which was usually provided for the layfolk who attended the services.

patron - the founder of a church or his successor, usually the principal land-owner of the area.

parish - the area served by a particular parish church.

piers - the vertical masonry supports of an arcade of arches.

precinct - the outer area around a monastic house containing the main religious and domestic buildings, and usually surrounded by a wall.

presbytery - the ceremonial area around the high altar of a church where the priests officiated.

prior - the head of a priory.

priory - a monastery headed by a prior, which might be an independent monastery, or might be subservient to an abbey.

pulpit - an elevated piece of liturgical furnishing from which sermons were preached.

rector/parson - the principal clergyman of a parish. Since most parishes were granted to some monastery or cathedral body, that body itself became the rector, and the spiritual needs of the parish were met by a vicar or a chaplain.

refectory - the eating hall of a religious house, usually on the opposite side of the cloister from the church.

religious orders - confederations of houses of monks, canons or friars. The chief orders represented in Fife were those of the Benedictine, Tironensian and Cistercian monks, the Augustinian canons, and the Dominican and Franciscan friars.

requiem mass - a mass offered on behalf of the soul of a dead person.

sacrament house - the locker where the bread consecrated at the mass could be stored until needed. It was usually to the north of the altar, and might be richly carved.

screens - medieval churches were subdivided into a variety of spaces, which might be enclosed by stone or timber screens. The main ones were those separating the choir from the nave, but they might also be found around the lesser altars within a church.

sedilia - the seats on the south side of the presbytery area where the clergy might sit at certain points of the services.

transept - the cross arms of a major church which contained additional altars and which gave it the characteristic cross shape preferred for important churches.

vaulting - the arched stone ceiling over parts of some buildings.

vicar - a deputy for the rector or parson of a parish, or for the canon of a cathedral.

window tracery - the decorative patterns of curved stone bars found at the head of many church windows.

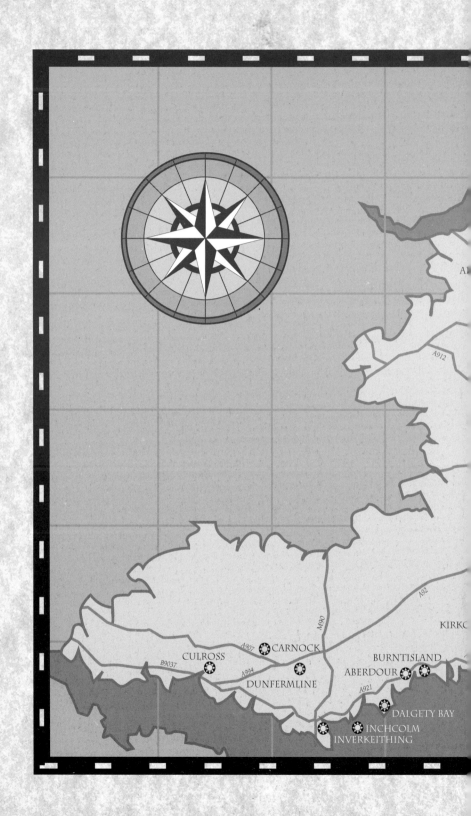

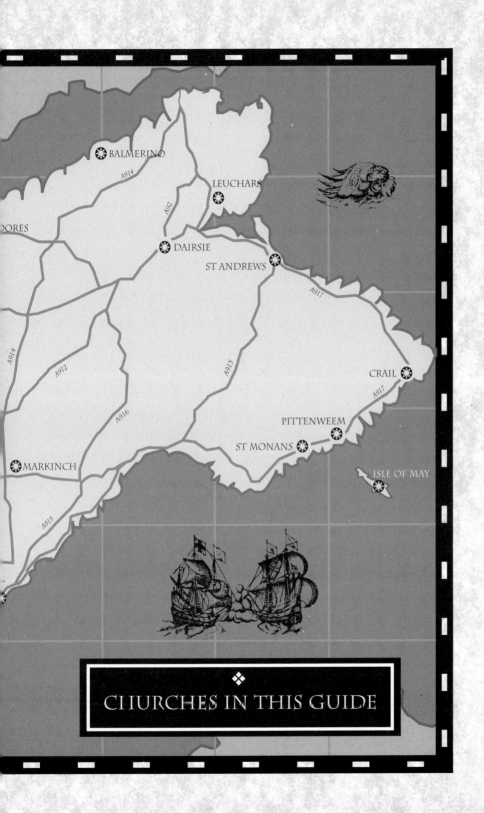

BALMERINO

A914

LEUCHARS

A92

DORES

DAIRSIE

ST ANDREWS

A917

A914

A912

A915

CRAIL

A917

A916

PITTENWEEM

ST MONANS

MARKINCH

ISLE OF MAY

A915

❖

CHURCHES IN THIS GUIDE

❖ ST ANDREWS, THE CHURCHES OF ST RULE AND ST MARY KIRKHEUGH

he early ecclesiastical community of Kinrimund probably had a number of churches within its boundaries. The earlier and more complete of the two which survive is the church of St Rule, a short way to the south-east of the ruins of the great cathedral.

St Rule's church now consists of a very tall tower with a square chamber to its east, and this probably represents the greater part of the church as originally built. This tall tower would have acted as a beacon for pilgrims, being visible from miles around. The lower part of the tower perhaps served as a small nave for the layfolk, with the east chamber housing the services of the clergy. Arches cut through both the east and west walls of this church show that it was later extended in both directions, though nothing of this survives above ground. These additions were probably made when Bishop Robert finally succeeded in introducing a community of Augustinian canons to St Andrews in the 1140s. Interestingly, it has been suggested that the architectural details of the inserted arches are so like those of a church at Wharram-le-Street in Yorkshire that the masons must have known each other's work. This is important, because Bishop Robert had originally been a canon at the priory of Nostell in Yorkshire, and Wharram was a church that belonged to that priory.

The date of the earlier parts of St Rule's is more problematic. The original layout is similar to that of the later eleventh century churches at Dunfermline and Restenneth (in Angus), and it has been suggested that St Rule's could also be of this date. However, the earlier parts are more likely to have been built by Bishop Robert, after he was appointed in 1123, but before he introduced the Augustinian canons.

The way that the three main streets of St Andrews point to the headland occupied by St Mary Kirkheugh suggests that this must have been the site of a very important early church, though it was later to be excluded from the cathedral precinct by a wall. The foundations of the church we now see, which were discovered through excavation in 1860, were built for Scotland's first college of priests, established in about 1249. These priests were the successors of the early clergy known as Culdees who had been associated with the cathedral, but did not wish to join the Augustinian community. They seem to have come to be regarded almost as a rival chapter to the Augustinians. For a time the church was even regarded as the Chapel Royal. The church was cross shaped, but probably only reached its final shape over an extended period. The longest part was the eastern limb which housed the choir for the clergy; it was extended at some unknown date to give their services a more spacious setting.

How to get there :-

OS sheet 59 NO 514 167 - St Rule's Church can be found within the St Andrews Cathedral precinct to the east of St Andrews town centre at the end of North Street. St Mary Kirkheugh lies to the north of the Cathedral, outwith the precinct wall and is well signposted. Parking is available around the town. The Cathedral is open throughout the year. Any further information can be obtained by calling Historic Scotland on 031 668 8600.

St Mary's is in the foreground

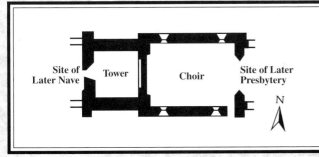

St Rule

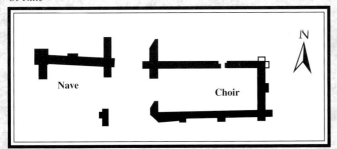

St Marys

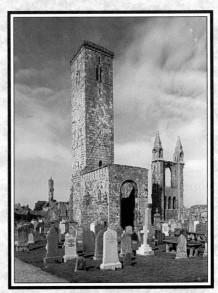

St Rule's

DUNFERMLINE ABBEY

t Margaret married Malcolm III in about 1070 in the royal residence at Dunfermline, and soon afterwards established the first community of monks in Scotland there. The monks were of the Benedictine order and came from Canterbury. The community probably died out in the chaos that followed Malcolm and Margaret's death in 1093, but their son, Edgar, re-established it some time after 1100. Excavations beneath the nave of the later abbey church in 1916 found traces of the older church built in two corresponding phases. The first building had a square tower-nave, with a rectangular choir on its east side (not unlike the first church of St Rule at St Andrews). Later a slightly larger choir was added, with a semi-circular apse to its east for the high altar. Fragments of the earlier structure can still be seen through a grating in the floor of the nave.

In about 1128 David I decided to expand his mother's foundation to create a full abbey, and yet more monks were brought from Canterbury, under the leadership of the prior of Canterbury himself. Since David's parents and six of his brothers were already buried in the church, the scale of the new building had to reflect the importance of what had become the mausoleum of the royal house of Scotland. For the earlier parts David almost certainly brought masons up from Durham, where the death of the bishop had resulted in a pause in operations. Dunfermline was only about half the size of Durham, although the carefully-proportioned design of its surviving nave gives a sense of scale way beyond its actual size. Originally built to a cross-shaped plan with three towers, it must have been by far the most impressive building raised in Scotland by that date. The eastern parts of this church were abandoned after the Reformation, and their site is now overlain by the parish church of 1818-1821. Projecting east of the modern church are fragments of the chapel which was added for the shrine of St Margaret shortly before 1250.

Dunfermline also has the substantial remains of a number of majestic monastic buildings, the main ones having been - as usual - laid out around the sides of a cloister on the south side of the church. Because of the steep slope of the land they had to be raised on vaulted undercrofts, which increase their magnificence. The earliest surviving parts are the lower storeys of the dormitory and latrine blocks, on the east side of the cloister, which are of the late thirteenth century. These survived the destruction of most of the monastic buildings by Edward I of England in 1303. The enormously impressive refectory hall on the south side of the cloister was being rebuilt with funds provided by Robert I (the Bruce) shortly before his death and subsequent burial in the abbey in 1329. Robert I probably also contributed to the equally impressive royal guest house, which was later extended as part of a palace for Queen Anne of Denmark, the wife of James VI. It was there that the future Charles I was born in 1600. On the north side of the precinct was the Abbot's House, which has recently been the subject of archaeological investigations in advance of its transformation into a major heritage centre.

How to get there :-

OS sheet 65 NT 088 873 - Dunfermline Abbey is situated in the centre of Dunfermline to the south of the High Street and is well signposted. Parking is available around the town. The Abbey is in the care of Historic Scotland and is open all year round. Any further information can be obtained by calling Historic Scotland on 0131 668 8600.

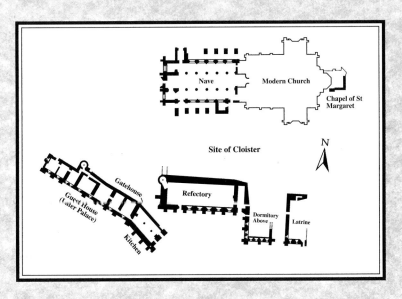

THE PARISH CHURCHES OF MARKINCH AND LEUCHARS

elatively few churches survive from the first phase of parochial development, although Fife is particularly fortunate to have parts of two notably fine churches dating from the first half of the twelfth-century.

The earlier of the two may be the west tower of the church at Markinch. We know there was a church here from at least the 1050s, because at that period it was granted by the bishop of St Andrews to the Culdees who lived on Loch Leven. But in the time of Bishop Robert (1123-59) it became a possession of St Andrews cathedral priory itself, and it was probably after then that the church was built. Although its architectural details show that it must be later than the tower of St Rule's Church at St Andrews, it does bear some resemblance to it . Perhaps all that can be safely said is that it was built by a mason who had been trained in the masons' lodges at St Andrews and who was familiar with St Rule's. The priory continued to take an architectural interest in their church up to the end of the middle ages, and the arms of Prior Hepburn, who died in 1522, have survived and are now re-set in the east wall of the church, which was rebuilt in 1786.

The other important Fife parish church of this period is at Leuchars. The first certain reference to the parish was between 1172 and 1187 when it was granted to St Andrews. However, the church was almost certainly built before then, and there is good reason to believe that masons brought to Dunfermline from Durham were responsible for much of the work. This would place the start of building around the second quarter of the twelfth century. Only the square choir and the rounded apse for the main altar survive from the original church; the existing nave is a rebuilding of the 1850s, while the apse has a slightly improbable bell tower perched on top of its stone vault. But these additions cannot obscure the extraordinary beauty and quality of the twelfth century architecture.

Internally there are two richly carved round-headed archways opening into the choir and the apse, and the detailing of the windows and vaulting of the apse are particularly fine. Unusually, the richest detailing is reserved for the outside, which gives the impression that the church has been turned inside out. The curved wall of the apse has two tiers of decorative arcading carried on paired shafts, the upper tier being the shorter of the two and embracing the small round-headed windows. The choir also has two tiers of decorative arcading, but the lower one is made even more elaborate by the intersecting of the arches with each other. Similar intersected arcading was also to be used for the lower internal walls of the presbytery and transepts at St Andrews Cathedral, though little now survives.

How to get there :-

Markinch: OS sheet 59 NO 297 019 - Markinch Parish Church lies north of the centre of Markinch village, east of Glenrothes. It can be reached by the B9130 which runs through Markinch, from which the church is clearly visible.

Leuchars: OS sheet 59 NO 455 214 - Leuchars parish Church can be found in the centre of Leuchars village, off the A919.

Both churches are still in use for public worship.

Markinch Church

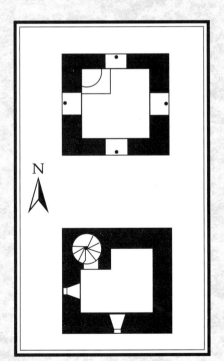

Leuchars External detail

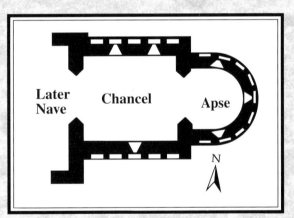

Plan of Markinch

Later Nave   Chancel   Apse

N

Plan of Leuchars

Leuchars Church

THE PARISH CHURCH OF
ABERDOUR

he small church dedicated to St Fillan at Aberdour is one of the most delightful in Fife. By the seventeenth century it was enclosed within the series of courtyards that spread out from the adjacent castle of the earls of Morton. To the parishioners of the time this must have provided a firm reminder of the twin powers of church and state that controlled their lives, while to modern eyes it adds greatly to the attractiveness of the setting.

From a charter of 1178 it appears that arrangements were made to grant the parish to the Augustinian priory of Inchcolm, and the church we now see may have been started in the mid-twelfth century. In the middle ages one of the canons of Inchcolm served as the parish priest. In its first stage the church had a simple rectangular chancel with a larger rectangular nave to the west. The interior was lit through small round-headed windows with wide splays towards the interior. At a later state an aisle was added along the south side, which opened into the nave through three wide arches. The date of this aisle is difficult to assess since its details are so simple, but it may have been of the later fifteenth or earlier sixteenth centuries. A large porch was also added over the main entrance for layfolk.

Many changes were made to the church after the Reformation. In 1588 the gables were reconstructed with crow steps, and a handsome belfry was placed at the apex of the west gable, which now contains a medieval bell from Dalgety. The traceried window beneath it is probably part of the same building campaign. Also added to the west wall is a fascinating text which reminds passers by of the need to answer for their sins before God. Later still aisles were added, with seating for the families above burial vaults. The aisle for the Phin of Whitehill family, which was added in 1608, still stands on the north side of the church. A more spacious vault and loft for the earls of Morton was inserted across the west end of the nave and aisle, which has since been removed; the porch was probably enlarged at the same time.

In 1790 the church was abandoned for a new one built in the centre of the village. However, in 1925 the decision was taken to bring the church back into use for worship, and it was carefully restored to the designs of William Williamson.

How to get there :-

OS sheet 66 NO 193 855 - The church lies just to the east of Aberdour Castle and can be reached by the A921, following signs for to the Silver Sands. The church is still in use for public worship.

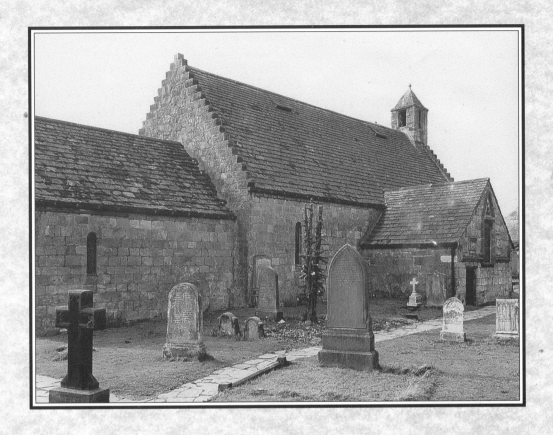

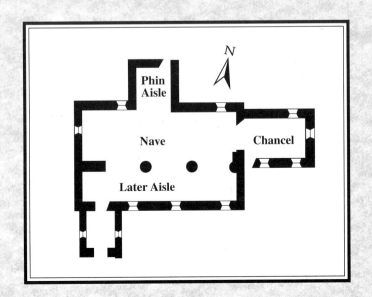

or centuries this was the largest building in Scotland. Its scale, along with its possession of the relics of one of Christ's apostles, reinforced Scotland's claim to be an independent European state. Without doubt, this size was also intended to reinforce the claims of St Andrews' bishops to be the most important in Scotland. St Rules was replaced as the cathedral church of St Andrews when Arnold began building operations during his short career as bishop between 1160 and 1162. The plan included an eastern arm of two unaisled and six aisled bays, and a nave that was planned to have fourteen aisled bays.

The complicated building history began when work was pressed ahead rapidly on the eastern arm. This was the part that contained the high altar and the choir stalls of the Augustinian canons, and it was important that they should be able to chant their daily services as soon as possible. This part was probably complete by 1238, when Bishop Malvoisin was buried within it. The nave was almost finished by the 1270s, but the new west gable was blown down in a gale - probably in 1272. Rebuilding of the western part of the nave to a slightly shortened plan may have been interrupted by the outbreak of the Wars of Independence in the 1290s, but it was ready for dedication as an act of national thanksgiving in 1318, in the presence of the great and good of the kingdom. Disaster struck again in 1378, when there was a great fire, and while rebuilding was still in progress the south transept gable collapsed in a gale in 1409.

As planned in the 1160s the new cathedral was the most important and ambitious piece of architecture in northern Britain of its period. In its own design it owed much to several buildings under construction in northern England, such as the Cistercian abbey of Kirkstall near Leeds. In its turn the cathedral was to be a major influence on many buildings on both sides of the Border, including the monastic churches at Jedburgh and Arbroath in Scotland and those of Hexham and Lanercost in England. Relatively little of St Andrews Cathedral now remains, though it is still possible to detect some of the design changes that were introduced as the work progressed, especially in the south wall of the nave. Careful examination of the east gable will reveal the original triple tiers of windows which lit and highlighted the relic chapel located behind the high altar. This sumptuously decorated area was the burial place of some bishops and archbishops some of whose graves can still be seen.

Attached to the church were the monastic buildings of the Augustinian community, which partly survive, while other parts were rebuilt by Lord Bute in the 1890s - apparently with the intention of installing a Catholic seminary within them. The most impressive of the monastic buildings is the wall that surrounded the precinct, much of which still stands, together with thirteen of its towers and four of the gates into the precinct. It dates from the fourteenth century, though it was heightened and strengthened in the early sixteenth century - a great monastery had to be prepared to defend its possessions!

How to get there :-

OS sheet 59 NO 515 167 - St Andrews Cathedral stands at the end of North Street, to the East of St Andrews town centre. Parking is well-signposted around the town. The Cathedral is in the care of Historic Scotland, and is open all year round. Any further information can be obtained by calling Historic Scotland on 0131 668 8600.

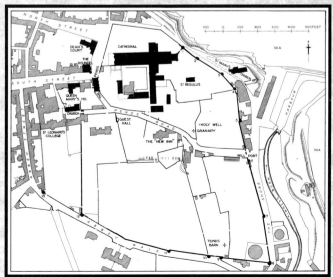

THE PRIORIES OF THE ISLE OF MAY AND PITTENWEEM

he small priory on the Isle of May has one of the most confusing histories of any religious house in Scotland. It was founded by David I in the mid-twelfth century, as a daughter-house of the great abbey of Reading in England, of which he had also become the patron. At that stage in its history Reading, and therefore the May, seems to have belonged to the Cluniac order, though both were later regarded as Benedictine. The priory was sold by Reading to St Andrews in the 1280's, changing its affiliation - yet again - from the Benedictine to the Augustinian order. As if such confusion were not enough, eventually the priory was transferred from the island site to its mainland estate at Pittenweem. This change was encouraged by repeated raids by English pirates in the early fourteenth century. One monk remained on the May however, to tend the shrine of St Ethernan and to welcome the many pilgrims.

Of the original priory on the Isle of May, the only upstanding remains are of the west range of the cloister. Patrick Learmonth, the owner of Dairsie Castle, converted this building into a house shortly before the Reformation, when a round tower was also added at one corner. Recent excavations led by Fife Regional Council have permanently revealed the remains of the church, along with the east range and the refectory on the south side of the cloister. The excavations are intended to illuminate the early history of the May and especially to search for evidence of St Ethernan and his followers who were reputedly murdered by the Vikings in 875. Some burials from this period have been found, and it is hoped that remains of an early monastery may yet be discovered.

When the priory was shifted to Pittenweem, it made use of an existing church that may have been built or remodelled in the later twelfth century. The surviving priory buildings, to the south of the church, date mainly from the later middle ages but have been extensively rebuilt since the Reformation. They include the precinct gate, and an attractive L-shaped grouping of buildings on the west and south sides of a courtyard. It is difficult to know if this represents the main cloister of the priory, or whether it was the outer courtyard of the precinct, with the cloister having been closer to the church. One interesting clue is a reference of 1549 to the 'little houses' of the canons, which may suggest that they were no longer living as communally as was once the case, and that there was no fully-formed cloister. Below the priory are the fascinating remains of a cave associated with St Fillan in the mists of the dark ages.

How to get there :-

Isle of May - A tourist boat service operates from Anstruther harbour, running daily trips (weather permitting) to the island during the summer months. For further information contact Anstruther (01333) 310103. Archaeological excavations are planned during August 1995 and 1996 when guided tours of the site will be provided. This is the only access to the Isle of May, which is designated as a National Nature Reserve, and is owned by Scottish Natural Heritage.

Pittenweem Church - The church lies in the centre of the village to the east of the Kirkgate and is still in use for public worship. The remains of the priory lie further down this road in Cove Wynd.

Isle of May Priory

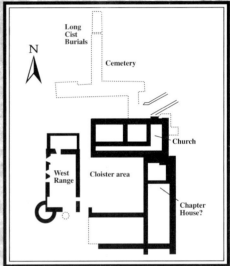

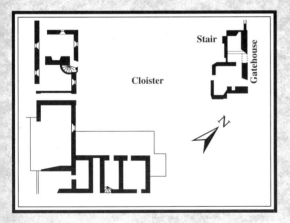

Pittenweem Priory in the late 18th Century

❖
LINDORES ABBEY

 he abbey of Lindores, near Newburgh, was founded in around 1190 by David, earl of Huntingdon, a grandson of David I. Its monks were Tironensians, an order that had a number of important houses in Scotland but was hardly represented elsewhere in the British Isles. The order had been a particular favourite of David I, and it is a sign of his great influence on the development of monasticism that the Tironensian Abbey he founded at Selkirk (later moved to Kelso), was the first house of the 'reformed' Benedictine religious orders to be established anywhere in Britain. Guido, the first abbot of Lindores, was brought from Kelso Abbey, and it was probably he who started the main building campaign. The poignant remains of two child-size stone coffins, which are sometimes said to have have belonged to Earl David's children, can be seen in the south transept.

The remains of the abbey are very fragmentary, though it is still possible to work out the basic layout. The church was built with a rectangular presbytery as the setting for the high altar. This was flanked by transepts (cross arms) with three chapels on the east side of each. The nave, which had the choir for the monks closest to the high altar, originally seems to have had no aisles. On the northern side of the west front can be seen a separate bell-tower which only touched the nave at one corner. An aisle was eventually added on the north side of the nave, though the position of the bell tower prevented it from extending the full length.

The cloister was on the south side of the church, and there are partial remains of the ranges on both its east and west sides, the best preserved being the east range next to the church. The slype, or parlour, still has its stone vaulting. This was the corridor which gave access from the cloister to the area of the precinct beyond it, usually containing the monks infirmary. This was the place where conversation could take place when necessary. Next to this is the shell of the chapter house, the business room of the monastery, which took its name from the daily reading of a chapter of the rule of St Benedict. Against the south wall of this are the remains of the stair that led to the cloister from the dormitory, which ran along this range at first-floor level. Traces of other, more outlying buildings are to be seen at various points around the abbey, especially the remains of a very large monastic barn in the fields to the south. The mill and mill-pond to the east are on the site of the abbey mill, and remind us of the important buildings which existed within the precinct.

How to get there :-

OS sheet 59 NO 243 184 - The Abbey lies to the east of Newburgh village c 100m to the east of the A913 from Cupar.The Abbey is in private ownership, and access is permitted courtesy of the owner. Parking is available in Newburgh.

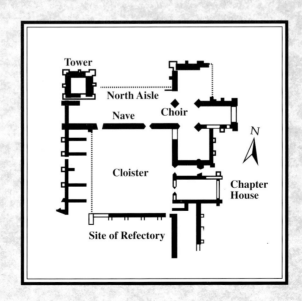

CULROSS ABBEY

ulross was the earlier of the two abbeys in Fife founded for the austere order of Cistercian monks. The order had been established at Citeaux in Burgundy (eastern France), but it was after St Bernard joined in about 1112 that enjoyed its greatest period of expansion. The first Cistercian house in Scotland was founded at Melrose in 1136. Culross was founded in about 1217 by Malcolm, earl of Fife as a daughter house of Kinloss in Moray, itself a daughter of Melrose.

In their attempt to return to the original principles of Benedictine monasticism, the early Cistercians turned their backs on the world as completely as possible, with the monks seldom leaving the precinct. Much of the physical work of the communities was carried out by illiterate lay brethren, in order to reduce contact with layfolk as much as possible. In view of this it is rather surprising that the Cistercians should have agreed to come to Culross, where there was already a township with its own parish church. The early cross shafts found at the abbey suggest that it was built on the site of the earlier community that is traditionally linked with St Serf.

The Cistercians tried to avoid architectural ostentation, and to achieve this a simple ground plan was copied at many of its churches. The altar was housed in a plain rectangular presbytery, to the west of which were transepts, with rectangular chapels on their eastern side. The western arm of these churches, which might have been expected to be the nave where layfolk could worship, was instead divided into two choirs: one for the monks

themselves and the other for the lay brethren. The church at Culross is one of the most complete examples of this type anywhere in Britain, even though much was lost at the Reformation and after.

Another great interest of the church is the survival of the stone screens which separated the two choirs. They were preserved incidentally when a tower was added over them by Abbot Andrew Masoun (1498-1513), despite the fact that the earlier Cistercians had discouraged the building of high bell towers. A post-Reformation tomb house was added off the north transept for the Bruce family, containing the highly ambitious monument made in 1625 for Sir George Bruce by the mason John Mercer.

To the south of the church are the remains of the monastic buildings around the cloister. Best preserved are parts of the west range, which housed the refectory and dormitory of the lay brethren. Also standing to a significant height are the lower parts of the east range undercroft, beneath the chapter-house, dormitory and latrine.

How to get there :-

OS sheet 65   NO 988 863 - Culross Abbey lies on the hill to the north of the village of Culross which is situated on the shores of the River Forth on the B9037. Parking is available in the village, from where the church and abbey can be reached via Mid-Causeway and Tanhouse Brae. The Abbey grounds are in the care of Historic Scotland and open all year round. The church, however, is still in use for public worship and separate access arrangements must be made.

BALMERINO ABBEY

he second of Fife's Cistercian abbeys was established at Balmerino, on the Tay coast, with monks from Melrose. It was founded in about 1227 by the widow of William the Lion, Queen Ermengarde, and their son, Alexander II. It is likely that the queen dowager planned it from the beginning as her own burial place, even though her husband had been buried in his own foundation for the Tironensian order at Arbroath.

Wherever possible monastic houses were laid out with the main buildings around a cloister on the south side of the church. Since the monks carried out many of their daily tasks within the covered walk-ways that ran around the edge of the cloister, having the church on the north meant that it did not block the light. This was an important consideration, as was usually the largest building of the group. At Balmerino, however, the cloister was on the north of the church, probably as the best water supply was on that side. This is a reminder that water, and the system of supply and drainage that depended on it, was one of the most important factors in the planning of a monastery.

The best preserved parts of the abbey are of the range on the east side of the cloister, though there are also fragments of what was probably the residence of the abbots and of a barn. But sections of the church walls also survive, and its overall plan has been discovered through excavation. From this we know that the church had a very similar layout to that at Culross, with two square chapels on each transept, to either side of a simple rectangular presbytery for the high altar, and with a long nave for the choirs of the monks and the lay brethren. However, at Balmerino - as at Lindores - the church was later enlarged by the addition of a single aisle on the side away from the cloister.

The east claustral range survives better than the rest of the abbey because it was converted into a house for the family to whom the monastic estates were granted after the Reformation. Before those changes the finest feature had been the chapter house; it was a square vaulted chamber against the east side of the range, which was approached through a vestibule. This arrangement allowed the chapter house to rise to a greater height than the presence of the first-floor dormitory would otherwise have allowed. Unfortunately, when it was converted into a house, the vault of the chamber itself was removed to allow the insertion of wooden floors, and chimney flues were broken through the vault of the vestibule.

How to get there :-

OS sheet 59 - NO 358 246 - Balmerino Abbey lies on the Tay coast c 3 miles west of Wormit and is clearly signposted. It is in the care of the National Trust for Scotland and is open to the public. For further information you should contact the Fife, Lothian and Borders Regional Office at 443 High St, Kirkcaldy, Tel 01592 266566.

Balmerino in 1837

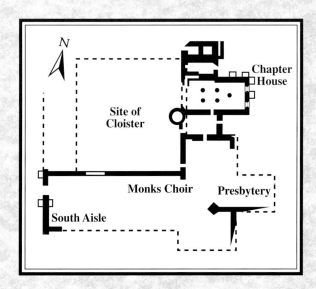

❖ CRAIL COLLEGIATE CHURCH

he survival here of an early cross slab suggests that there was a focus of Christian worship in Crail from the earliest times. The church we now see may have been started around the mid-twelfth century by Ada, countess of Northumberland and Huntingdon, who was the mother of both Malcolm IV and William the Lion. She granted the church and its income to the Cistercian nunnery she founded at Haddington in East Lothian. When a parish church was granted to some other religious institution in this way, that institution became the nominal 'rector' of the parish, and received the greater part of its ecclesiastical income. The institution would then usually appoint a vicar or a chaplain to look after the spiritual welfare of the parishioners.

At Crail the earliest surviving part is the chancel, which was first built as a small rectangle around the mid-twelfth century, and much of its north wall still survives. A nave was probably built as part of the same operation, but in the first half of the thirteenth century it was rebuilt on a much larger scale. In doing this the main space of the nave was both widened and lengthened, and aisles were placed on each side, separated from the main space by arcades carried on five cylindrical columns. Above the arcades the walls rose higher than the flanking aisles and were pierced by small windows to create what is known as a clearstorey. The nave was given additional emphasis by a bell tower capped by a spire at its west end, and at some stage a porch was built over the main entrance for the layfolk.

The church was further enlarged at various periods. At least one chapel was added against the nave, and the original chancel was extended eastwards. One reasons for the extension of the chancel was the formation of the clergy into a college in 1517 under the leadership of a provost. Two of the priests in the college were attached to the altar of St Mary, two to the altar of St Michael, and others to the altars of St James, St Nicholas, St Bartholomew, St John the Apostle, the Holy Cross and another altar dedicated to the Virgin. There may later have been priests attached to altars of St Stephen and St Katherine. This reminds us that Crail was a thriving burgh. It also demonstrates that such a church could have a large number of altars and associated priests, whose main task was to offer up prayers for the souls of the dead.

Since the Reformation the church has undergone many changes, including the removal of the chapels and porch, and the shortening of the chancel. But the most dramatic change was in 1815, when the outer walls of the aisles were rebuilt. At the same time a single roof was placed over both the main space and the flanking aisles of the nave, replacing the individual roofs. More recently, in 1963, a careful restoration has re-exposed a number of the medieval features.

How to get there :-

OS sheet 59 NO 613 079 - Crail Church is situated off the A917, on the north side of the Marketgate. The church is still in use for public worship.

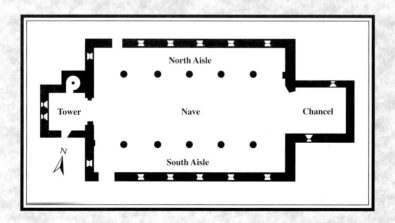

Culross Abbey

St Andrews Cathedral

Dunfermline Abbey

CARNOCK PARISH CHURCH

arnock was probably built around 1200, the first reference to it dating from the time of Bishop Malvoisin of St Andrews (1202-38), who granted it to the hospital at Loch Leven. It eventually belonged to the priory of Trinitarians at Scotlandwell, from which one of the brethren would have acted as parish priest for the layfolk of Carnock. Although only small, the church was a handsomely proportioned structure with small pointed windows which splayed widely towards the interior. A pair of those windows in the east wall gave particular prominence to the high altar, and there were single windows in the side walls, though most of those have been greatly enlarged. This was probably in 1602, when Sir George Bruce, the local landowner, is known to have carried out a great deal of rebuilding. (This is the same Sir George whose magnificent tomb is still to be seen at Culross Abbey.)

As in so many cases, the medieval church was eventually abandoned for worship when a newer and more conveniently planned one was built nearby. At Carnock the new church was completed in 1840.

How to get there :-

OS sheet 65   NT 043 891 - Carnock church can be found in the village of Carnock on the north side of the A907, 4 miles west of Dunfermline. The ruins lie within the grounds of the new parish church which is clearly visible from the road.

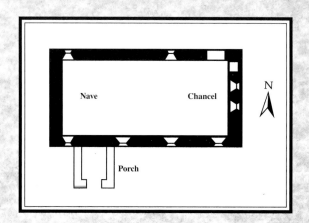

❖
ABDIE PARISH CHURCH

ike Carnock, Abdie was built as a rectangular structure, though on a considerably larger scale. The church was granted to nearby Lindores Abbey shortly before 1200 by David, Earl of Huntingdon, who probably founded both abbey and parish, although the church may not have been built until several decades later. Indeed, it may not have been built by the time of Bishop de Bernham's dedication to St Magridin, which took place on 5 September 1242.

Despite the simplicity of its plan Abdie is a fine building. Particular emphasis is given to the position of the high altar at the east end by the closer concentration of buttresses and the grouping of three lancets (single pointed windows) in the east wall. The parish priest had his own doorway which can still be seen on the south side of the chancel and the screen between the chancel and nave would have been to the west of this. But there are also corbels (projecting blocks) for a beam immediately in front of the altar, and it is possible that this could have been for suspending the veil that screened the altar from view during Lent.

The church was altered in various ways both before and after the Reformation, in order to meet changing needs. Windows were enlarged and a porch was added over the main entrance. The greatest change, however, was the addition in 1661 of an aisle for Sir Robert Balfour, of Denmylne Castle. The church was eventually abandoned for worship when a new one was completed in 1827.

A fascinating group of sculpted stones can be found in the 18th century carriage shed, beside the entrance to the churchyard. These include a late medieval tomb effigy of a cleric, and a Pictish symbol stone.

How to get there :-

OS sheet 59 NO 259 163 - Abdie Parish church lies to the south west of Lindores on the opposite shore of Lindores Loch. Turn south west off the A913 towards Grange of Lindores, and turn south east after crossing the railway bridge. The tomb effigies and the Pictish symbol stone can be found in an open-fronted shed by the road. There is no formal parking and care should be taken not to block the road.

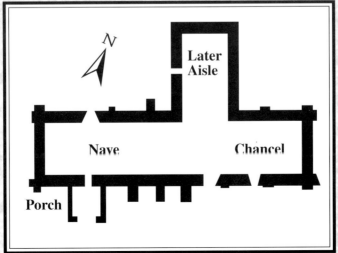

❖
INVERKEITHING FRIARY

he two main orders of friars, the Franciscans (the Grey Friars) and the Dominicans (the Black Friars), were both given formal recognition in 1215. They each represented an attempt to follow a way of life imitating that of the apostles, in which the friars possessed no property of their own, but lived simply off the offerings of the faithful. They were known as mendicants from the Latin word meaning beggar, and they especially concentrated on missionary activity in the towns, where the growth of heresy was regarded as a particular problem. Both orders reached Scotland in the early 1230s, and set about establishing themselves in the main burghs. It is sometimes said that the Franciscans had reached Inverkeithing by 1268, though the first definite reference was in 1384.

Difficulties arose in the order concerning their refusal to own property, and the Franciscans were particularly prone to quarrelling over the ethical problems this posed. But by the time Inverkeithing was built, they were clearly prepared to construct quite grand buildings. Indeed, Inverkeithing has the grandest friars' building to survive anywhere in Scotland. The buildings of the friary were laid out around a large cloister-like open space, and three vaults together with some foundations survive on its north side. The most splendid surviving structure, however, is thought to have been the guest house, on the west side of the cloister. Since the friary was in the burgh with the northern port of the Queen's Ferry across the Firth of Forth, the guest house is likely to have been frequently used by travellers, and a large building was needed. It is sometimes suggested that Queen Annabella, the wife of Robert III, died here in 1401.

Much of the building that remains dates either from alterations of the period after the Reformation or from a campaign of restoration in the 1930s, though the basic arrangements are probably authentic. The main guest hall was above a vaulted basement, which had a passage running through to the cloister behind. The hall itself was approached by a stone forestair. At one end of this block is a smaller second block with chambers on its upper floors. Despite the alterations, it still offers the clearest picture in Scotland of how the domestic buildings of a medieval friary would have looked.

How to get there :-

OS sheet 65 NT 110 822 - Inverkeithing Friary lies on the High Street in the centre of the town and now houses Inverkeithing Museum. The Museum is open Wednesday to Sunday, 11am - 5pm. For further details contact 01383 410495.

❖

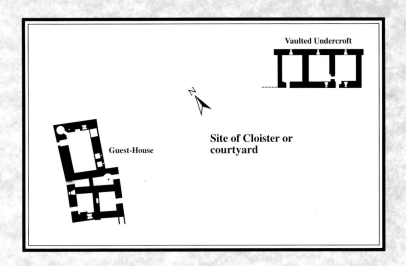

Vaulted Undercroft

Guest-House

Site of Cloister or
courtyard

N

41

ST MONANS CHURCH

ife has many beautiful churches, but that at St Monans must be regarded as one of the most attractive, both as a piece of architecture, and in its setting by the sea on the edge of this fishing village. It was first built between 1362 and 1370 by David II, as an act of thanksgiving to St Monan. The king was wounded at Nevilles Cross and one of the arrowheads could not be extracted until David went on a pilgrimage to St Monan. As he prayed, the arrowhead miraculously leapt out.

The shell of the church probably dates from the 1360's. It was set out to a cross-shaped plan, though it is uncertain if the western arm of that cross, the nave, was ever built. Rising above the crossing is a stumpy tower with a spire. Internally, a particularly attractive original feature dating from the fourteenth century is the sedilia, the stone seats to the south of the site of the high altar. A full set of medieval consecration crosses survive on the walls of the choir.

In 1471 the decision was taken by James III to establish a small community of Dominican friars at the church. This was probably not so much from motives of piety, but because he was anxious that Scotland should be recognised as an autonomous province by the Dominican order, and there was a need for another friary to justify this. The community was never a large one, possibly never having more than two friars at any one time. Nevertheless, it seems there may have been quite extensive rebuilding around 1471, extending to both the windows and the handsome stone vaulting above the choir.

After the Reformation the nave - if it was ever built - and the transepts were eventually abandoned, with only the choir being retained for worship. But in the course of several restorations the transepts were again brought back into use. The church now functions well with the pulpit and communion table below the tower, and the three arms spreading out around them, though this means that the congregation faces west and not east, as originally intended.

How to get there :-

St Monans church lies on the west side of St Monans off the A917 and is clearly visible from the road. It is still in use for public worship, and a large car park is provided by the churchyard gates.

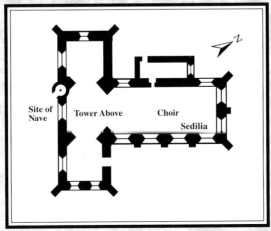

❖
INCHCOLM ABBEY

he island of Inchcolm, in the Firth of Forth, was a retreat for religious men over a long period and part of a cross slab, possibly of the ninth century, has been found here. There is also a memorial of the type known as a hog-back, because of its shape, which may mark a viking grave of the tenth century. By the eleventh century there were hermits here, and when the storm-bound Alexander I in 1123 was given shelter by one of them, he vowed to establish a community of Augustinian canons on the island. The hermit's cell that sheltered him is said to be represented in the small vaulted structure to the north-west of the abbey church, although it has been extensively rebuilt.

Alexander was probably unable to fulfil this vow before his death in 1124, and it was left to David I to carry out his wishes. The small church of two rectangular compartments that was built some time around the second quarter of the twelfth century is still recognisable, though it was later greatly extended. Around 1200 a new choir was built, and a tower raised above the original one. Two screens were constructed at the base of that tower to separate the choir of the canons from the nave of the layfolk, and the counterpoint between the two arches of one screen and the three arches of the other must have been particularly attractive. Further additions during the thirteenth century included a beautiful octagonal chapter house - one of only three known to have been built in Scotland. The choir of the church was again extended by Bishop Richard of Dunkeld in 1265. At the same time the body of one of his predecessors was reburied in the choir, and a recess with fine paintings that is still to be seen may have been part of this.

The fourteenth century was a turbulent period for the abbey, and it was only in the time of Abbots Lawrence (1394-1417) and Walter Bower (1418-49) that peace and the possibility of renewed building activity returned. Abbot Walter was a particularly important figure, being the author of the famous history of Scotland, the *Scotichronicon*. It was probably in their time that the church and most of the monastic buildings were reconstructed. Oddly enough, the old church was allowed to remain, with the cloister being built on its southern flank. The new church was built to the east of the old one.

Although they are unusual in a number of ways, the new monastic buildings of Inchcolm are the most complete anywhere in Scotland, and provide the clearest idea of what a medieval Scottish monastery looked like. The stone-vaulted walks around the cloister occupy the whole of the ground floor of the buildings, with the old church serving as the fourth walk. Above the east walk is the dormitory of the canons, with a sea-washed latrine at its outer end. Above the south walk is the refectory, while above the west range was perhaps a guest house. A range that was probably the residence of the abbot projected at right angles from the end of the dormitory, to which it was connected by the latrine block.

How to get there :-

OS sheet 66 NT 189 826 - Boat trips are run during the summer season from North and South Queensferry. For further details of sailing times please contact the operators as shown below.

The Heather, village pier, North Queensferry - 0131 554 6881/ 0374 103405. The Maid of the Forth, Hawes Pier, South Queensferry - 0506 852296

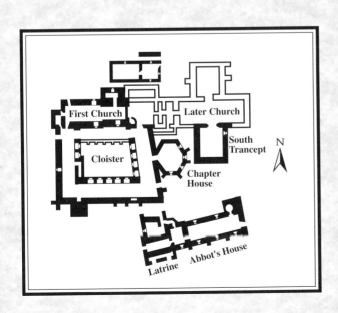

ST ANDREWS, HOLY TRINITY PARISH CHURCH

mong the finest buildings of the later Middle Ages were the parish churches of the greater burghs, which often came to be regarded as a particular focus of civic pride. At St Andrews the parish church had originally been within the cathedral precinct, and had been a possession of the priory since about 1163. But in 1410 Sir William Lindsay of the Byres presented a site at the heart of the burgh for a new church, where the parishioners might be less under the control of the cathedral priory. Archaeological excavations in 1992 have shown that a row of timber houses had to be demolished to make way for the church, and the tenants evicted. The new church may have taken nearly twenty years to build and Prior James Bisset seems to have contributed towards the building of the choir, which was the financial responsibility of the Cathedral Priory.

The new church was a large rectangle of nine bays in length, with an aisle along each side, and a spired tower rising above its north-west corner. Altars were progressively founded within the church, at which prayers could be said for their founders. Eventually there may have been over thirty such altars within Holy Trinity, some of which would have served as guild altars for the trades of the burgh. Many would have been set up within the aisles or against the piers that carried the arches separating the main body of the church from the aisles. But for other altars special chapels were built against the flanks of the church, giving it a more irregular outline than had originally been intended. Most of the rich furnishings which created the setting for medieval worship were lost after John Knox's fiery sermon of 1559, while many of the architectural features were swept away in a major rebuilding of 1798-1800. An altogether different appearance was created in a wholesale restoration by Peter MacGregor Chalmers between 1907 and 1909.

Following the rebuilding and later restoration, the main surviving parts of the original church are the north-western tower and spire, together with parts of the arcade arches. But in spite of all the changes it has undergone there are still many interesting features inside the church, including two of the early sixteenth century stalls that would have been occupied by the clergy during their services in the choir. Perhaps the most impressive feature to be seen is the enormous monument to Archbishop James Sharp, who was murdered in 1679 by a group of covenanters who could not forgive him for having abandoned his own covenanting views.

How to get there :-

OS sheet 59 NO 509 167 - Holy Trinity Church lies on South Street, St Andrews and is in use for public worship. Parking is available around the town.

Medieval tower and arcade arches preserved during rebuilding 1907-09

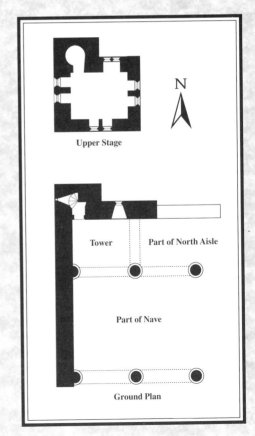

Upper Stage

N

Tower   Part of North Aisle

Part of Nave

Ground Plan

ST ANDREWS, THE COLLEGIATE CHURCH OF ST SALVATOR

he people of the late Middle Ages were acutely conscious of their own sinfulness, and of the need to obtain forgiveness if they were to escape damnation. It was believed that this forgiveness could be obtained by arranging for requiem masses to be said after death. This could be done by leaving money to pay for a certain number of masses to be said immediately after death, and perhaps on the anniversary of death. Another way was to belong to a guild or trade confederation of some kind, most of which arranged for prayers for the souls of their members. But some of the most wealthy members of society established colleges of clergy, in which it was intended that prayers would be offered for their souls till the end of time. The founders of these colleges often provided for additional charitable functions, and in a university city such as St Andrews, these functions were likely to be educational.

St Salvator's college was one of these, and was founded by Bishop James Kennedy in 1450. The chapel he built is largely complete, though it has lost its stone vault and the original window tracery. Despite these losses, it is a fascinating building, particularly in showing how Kennedy was influenced by what he had seen on the continent. The plan of the chapel was an elongated rectangle, with a polygonal eastern apse as the setting for the high altar. This was perhaps the first example of

such an apse to be introduced into Scotland, though it was to be copied in several other churches. In this case the idea was probably taken from France, especially since we know that the college's exquisite silver mace was made in Paris for Kennedy by no less a craftsman than Jean Mayelle, the silversmith of the heir to the French throne.

Within the chapel the most delightful feature is Kennedy's own tomb, to the north of the altar. Although badly damaged, the quality of the delicate stonework of the tomb canopy is still apparent, while the recess within the tomb was decorated with miniature architectural detailing. A position to the north of the altar was a favourite spot for the tomb of a church's founder. This was perhaps because in this situation it could also serve as a Tomb of Christ or Easter Sepluchre, where the consecrated host could be symbolically entombed between Good Friday and Easter Sunday. Next to Kennedy's tomb is a handsome sacrament house, where bread consecrated at the mass could be stored for use on other occasions.

How to get there :-

OS sheet 59 NO 509 168 - St Salvator's Church can be found on the north side of North Street on the south side of the University quadrangle. It is open on a regular basis, and further information can be sought from the Head Janitors Office, St Andrews University. phone 01334 476161.

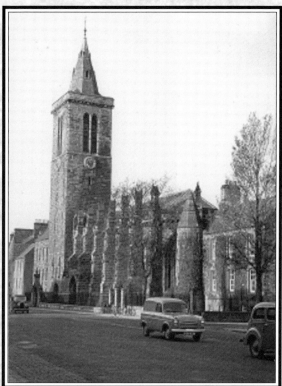

Bishop Kennedy's tomb.

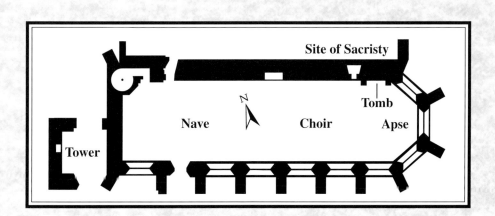

ST ANDREWS, THE COLLEGIATE CHURCH OF ST LEONARD

he motives behind the foundation of the college of St Leonard at St Andrews were similar to those we have already seen at St Salvator's Collegiate Church. In this case the college was founded by Archbishop Stewart and Prior Hepburn in 1512, though the religious use of the site has a much longer history than that. There seems to have been a hospital run by Culdees here before 1144, because in that year it was decided it should be used as hostel for pilgrims and visitors. Later it became a refuge for old women and poor men, perhaps because the number of pilgrims coming to St Andrews was declining. When the college was eventually founded it also housed novices of the Augustinian order who were receiving a university education, and was originally closely under the control of the adjacent cathedral priory. Around the time of the foundation of the college the existing chapel was extended, and a tower, a sacristy and a porch were added to it.

After the Reformation the chapel continued to be used by the college, though it also served as a parish church. But in 1747, at a time when the fortunes of the university were at a low ebb, the colleges of St Salvator's and St Leonard's were united, and eventually in 1761 the chapel ceased to be used for worship altogether. After this it suffered major losses, including the demolition of its tower. There was further damage in 1853, when the principal of the United Colleges of the University created a carriage drive through what had been the western part of the church, and cobbled together the present make-shift facade. As a result of all of this, the chapel is now only a fragment of what was once there. However, following its re-roofing in 1910 and its careful restoration between 1948 and 1952 it is still possible to appreciate something of its original architectural qualities. Plans are presently under consideration to make further improvements to the chapel.

How to get there :-

OS sheet 59 NO 512 166 - St Leonard's Chapel lies within the grounds of St Leonard's School and can be reached by walking west from the Pends into the College. Access can be arranged by appointment with the St Mary College Janitor, phone 01334 476161.

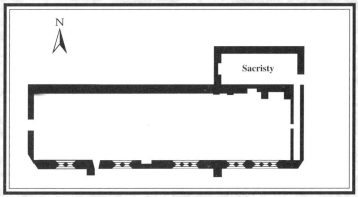

❖ DYSART PARISH CHURCH

lthough the majority of Scottish parish churches were of simple rectangular plan, as at Abdie, more complex churches were still being built in the wealthier parts of the country. Since the coastal fringes of Fife were among the richer areas of Scotland, many of its churches were highly ambitious buildings. One of the most impressive of these was at Dysart, though it has been a ruin since its replacement by a new building in 1802, and the site of the south aisle is now covered by the road down to the harbour.

The name Dysart may be derived from word a, meaning a desert or place of solitude, and there is a cave near the church (now in the grounds of a Carmelite nunnery) which is traditionally associated with St Serf. This suggests that there could be a long tradition of Christian worship around the site of the present church, though the building we now see dates mainly from the fifteenth century.

In its final form the main body of the church was a large rectangle, with an aisle on each side running the full length of both nave and chancel, as at the parish church of St Andrews. However, it is clear from changes in the masonry and of the design of the surviving arcade piers that the church only achieved this form at the end of a long architectural development. The parish was eventually granted to the college of St Mary Kirkheugh in St Andrews, though it seems that at one stage there may have been a proposal to found a college at Dysart itself. This was presumably the idea of the later landholders, the powerful Sinclair family, who already had a collegiate chapel at their principal residence of Roslin in Midlothian.

The most impressive feature of the church was a tower, which projected southwards from the west bay of the south aisle, and which had a porch over the main entrance against its east face. This tower rises through eight storeys to a remarkable height of about 22.5 metres, and the top storey seems to have been habitable, since it has a fireplace. Rather unusually for a church, the two lower storeys of the tower - which were both vaulted - were designed to be defensible, having shot-holes for hand-held guns. Some of the architectural details are like those at nearby Ravenscraig Castle, and it has been suggested that the church tower was built around the same time as the castle. Ravenscraig was started in 1460, for James II and Queen Mary of Guelders.

How to get there :-

OS sheet 59 NO 302 931 Dysart Church and harbour are just to the east of Kirkcaldy, on the east side of the A955 from Kirkcaldy, past Beveridge Park.

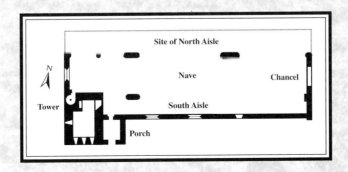

Inchcolm Abbey

St Monans Church

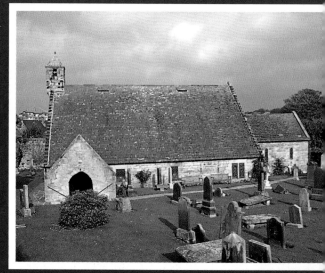

Aberdour Church

Dunfermline Abbey

KIRKCALDY PARISH CHURCH

he parish of Kirkcaldy existed by the time of David I (1124-53), during whose reign it was granted to Dunfermline Abbey. This grant was later confirmed by Bishop Robert of St Andrews and Pope Alexander III in 1163. In the early thirteenth century, however, there was an attempt to suggest that the church was simply a chapel within Dysart parish. But this was eventually resolved, and Bishop William of St Andrews (1202-38) made arrangements for vicars to be provided, while Dunfermline Abbey continued to receive the major part of the parochial income.

Some years later, on 24 March 1245, Bishop David de Bernham carried out one of his many consecrations and from what we know of its plan before rebuilding in the early nineteenth century, it is possible much of the medieval church existed by then. There was a nave of four bays with an aisle along each side, and a long rectangular chancel. It also had a western tower, which is the only part of the medieval church to survive, and which has all the hallmarks of being a late medieval addition. One possible clue to its date is the bell, which was originally cast in 1553. Since bells were often provided once building work was nearing completion, this may indicate the approximate date of the tower.

After the Reformation the church was extended in many ways. Porches were added in 1618 and 1764, and external stairs to the inserted lofts in 1648 and 1656, though the greatest single addition was an asymmetrical aisle on the north side, which gave the church a T-shaped plan. Such plans came to be highly favoured in the Scottish reformed church because they allowed a clear view of a pulpit against the centre of the south wall from all three arms. Perhaps this addition can be dated to 1643, when the master mason John Mylne was admitted as a burgess of Kirkcaldy.

In 1806 the decision was taken to rebuild the church, and the distinguished architects Archibald and James Elliot were commissioned to do this. They submitted two plans, one of which was for an octagonal building, but it was decided to build to the present rectangular plan. A later minister did not approve of the decision to retain the old tower - in 1845 the Rev. John Alexander suggested that 'it must indicate to strangers either a scarcity of money, or a want of taste in the inhabitants'. The gallery in the new church seems to have caused problems from the start, and in 1812 a report was prepared on strengthening it. But in 1828, when an enormous congregation crowded into the church to hear the famous preacher Edward Irving, part of it collapsed, killing twenty eight people

How to get there :-

OS sheet 59 NT 280 917 - Kirkcaldy Parish Kirk is situated in the town centre of Kirkcaldy, just off Kirk Wynd and parking is well sign-posted around the town. The church is still in use for public worship.

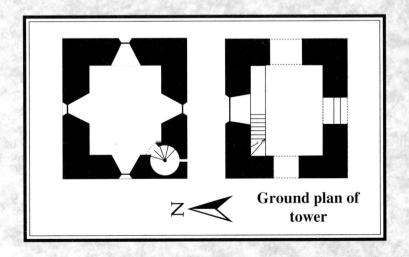

Ground plan of
tower

ST ANDREWS, THE CHURCH OF THE DOMINICANS

he Dominican friars, also known as the Black Friars and the Friars Preachers, were founded in 1215 by St Dominic, at Toulouse in southern France. They probably reached Scotland about fifteen years later, and at their height had sixteen Scottish friaries. They are said to have had a house at St Andrews by the 1270s, though there is no certainty of one there before the 1460s. The order placed great stress on academic learning as a way of combating heresy, and was naturally attracted to the universities may have been the growth of St Andrews which attracted them in the mid-fifteenth century.

In 1514 it was decided that money left to the order by Bishop Elphinstone of Aberdeen should be used for rebuilding the friary at St Andrews. Unfortunately, very little is known about this operation as only a single chapel that projected from the north side of the church survives - though that is a highly interesting fragment in itself.

Like the east end of St Salvator's Chapel, the chapel of the Blackfriars' church is a polygonal apse. Such sideward-projecting apses had already been built at other Scottish churches by the early sixteenth century, with examples at the churches of Ladykirk (Berwickshire) and Arbuthnott (Kincardineshire). At St Andrews it is possible that the idea was borrowed from the Low Countries. The Scottish Dominicans had close contacts with their brethren in the the Low Countries and we know they had recently been revitalised by a visit from them. It is also important to note that the window tracery, with its simple loop-like forms, is likely to have been inspired by examples in the Low Countries.

As in the earlier work at St Salvator's chapel in St Andrews, we are reminded that Scottish patrons and masons in the later Middle Ages were prepared to draw inspiration from a surprisingly wide range of sources at home and abroad to produce buildings that satisfied their aesthetic requirements. Nevertheless, there are elements in the design of the chapel that are strongly Scottish in character, such as its tunnel-shaped stone vault with a surface application of ribs.

How to get there :-

OS sheet 59 NO 507 165 - The remains of the chapel lie in the grounds of Madras College and are open to public access. They are cared for by Historic Scotland.

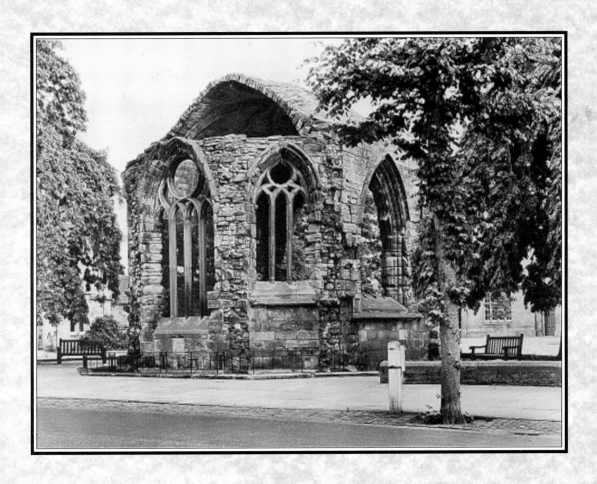

BURNTISLAND AND DAIRSIE CHURCHES

s well as its fine complement of medieval buildings, Fife has two of the most important of the few churches to be built in the decades following the Reformation in Scotland. The earlier of the two, at Burntisland, was under consideration by about 1589, and work started in earnest about three years later. Its plan is a complete rejection of the medieval tradition, being a square in which aisles surround a central square space on all four sides. The central square, defined by four piers at its corners, rises through the middle of the church and is expressed externally as a tower, which was rebuilt to the form we now see in 1749. Extra seating was provided within the aisles by galleries, which were inserted in the early seventeenth century.

A church laid out to such a plan was clearly intended to allow all members of the congregation to be as close to the preacher as possible; the communion table was also placed at the centre, below the tower, rather than at the far end of an axial vista. It has been suggested that such a centralised plan owes something to prototypes in the Low Countries. However, it seems more likely to represent a particularly Scottish solution to the problem of designing churches at a time when Scotland was going through one of its more Protestant phases.

The second of these two churches is at Dairsie, where Archbishop John Spottiswood of St Andrews owned the castle for a time. There had been a parish church adjacent to the castle since at least the 1160s, but in 1621 the archbishop decided to rebuild it as a model of what a church fitted for reformed episcopalian worship should be.

Significantly, it had been only three years earlier that the Perth Assembly passed the strongly Anglican five articles, in deference to the known wishes of James VI. The views of Scotland's bishops were in the ascendant at that time.

Like a majority of its medieval predecessors in Scotland, Dairsie was a buttressed aisle-less rectangle, and the tracery of the windows consciously imitated designs in medieval churches. As a sign of its modernity and relevance to its own period, however, it was also given a handsome classical frontispiece to the entrance, and a fine bell turret was built out at one angle. Internally, the church was arranged on traditional lines, with the communion table on an elevated platform at the east end, separated from the rest of the church by a screen. But the future within the Scottish church was not to be as the archbishop would have wished, and much of this internal arrangements was swept away following a disapproving report by the presbytery in 1648, during the period of the Civil War.

How to get there :-

Burntisland - OS Sheet 66 NT 233 587 St Columba's Church in Burntisland can be found on East Leven St, on the south side of the town. The church is still in use for public worship.

Dairsie - OS sheet 59 NO 414 161 Dairsie Church lies to the south of Dairsie village off the A91(T). Turn off at the sign for Pitscottie and follow this road for about a half mile. The church is on the right hand side above the River Eden. The church is no longer in use for public worship, and is now owned by the St Andrews Preservation Trust.

Burntisland Church

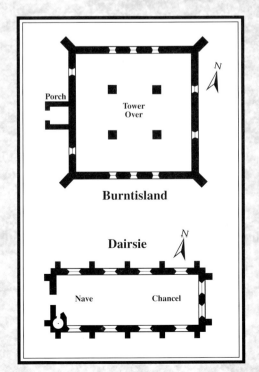

Dairsie Church

DALGETY, ST BRIDGET

St Bridget's is a medieval church that was modified for post-Reformation worship in a way that clearly illustrates how old buildings could be adapted to new practices. The medieval church at Dalgety had been granted to Inchcolm Abbey by William the Lion at some date between 1165 and 1178, and it seems likely that canons from there looked after the needs of the medieval parishioners. It may have been one of the first churches in Fife that was built as an aisle-less rectangular structure, though there is little to indicate the precise date of construction.

The most interesting aspect of the church, which survives only as a ruined shell since being replaced by a new building in 1829, is the post-Reformation alterations. We have seen how many medieval churches had chapels added around their walls, where the wealthier parishioner could be buried and have prayers said for their souls at altars close to their tombs. This practise of building aisles continued in many churches after the Reformation, especially once burial within the church itself was forbidden, as already seen at Aberdour. Many wealthier families chose to have a rectangular burial aisle built against the wall of the church; their dead would be buried within vaults below the aisle, while the family would take part in the Sunday worship from a pew or a loft within the aisle. Of course, prayers could no longer be offered for the dead within the Reformed church, but these aisles in many ways perpetuated the plans of medieval chantry chapels in their relationship to the main body of the church. Indeed, some chantries were adapated to serve as family aisles.

Dalgety came to be particularly well-provided with family aisles. The earliest may have been two symmetrically arranged structures on each side of the church, which gave the church a Greek-cross-shaped plan at one stage. However, these were both later rebuilt, and another was added on the north. But the most magnificent of the aisles added to the medieval church is that built at the west end for the first earl of Dunfermline, the Chancellor of Scotland, who died in 1622. It is an L-shaped, two-storeyed building, the lower floor of which contained two burial vaults, while the upper level had two very handsomely appointed rooms. Within the larger of the two rooms the family could sit in comfort to listen to the service, and between the services they could retire to the inner room to take a meal, with the added comfort of a fireplace!

The arrangements at Dalgety are particularly interesting as a reflection of post-Reformation planning, though the ruins today are only a shadow of their former glory. The greatest loss is the woodwork that would have been a particularly prominent feature. Against the south wall would have been the pulpit, with the communion table in front of it. There may also have been a close concentration of pews across the floor of the church. But perhaps the greatest impact would have been made by the galleries - known as lofts - which we know existed at both the east and west ends. That at the east end, where the chancel had been in the medieval church, was reached by an external stone stair, while that at the west opened off Chancellor Dunfermline's loft, and would have been originally emphasised by highly enriched carving.

How to get there :-

OS Sheet 66 NT 169 838 The church of St Bridget's is in the care of Historic Scotland. The church can be found close to the shore on the east side of Dalgety Bay off the A921 and is clearly signposted.

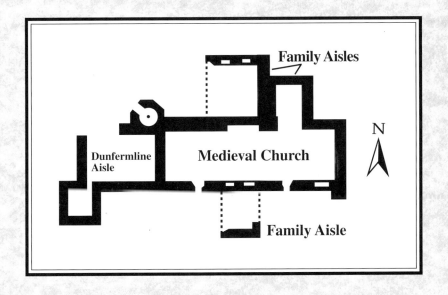

FIFE
CHARTER FOR THE ENVIRONMENT

This booklet is produced as part of the Fife Charter for the Environment Action Programme with the intention of raising the awareness of Fife's rich natural and cultural heritage. The Environmental Charter sets out the Regional Council's approach to tackling environmental issues. It provides a framework for future action by everyone, as each one us has a responsibility for looking after and improving our local environment.

WHO TO CONTACT

Should you wish copies of the Charter or require any further information, please contact. Grace MacDonald or Andy Hills at:

Department of Economic
Development & Planning,
Fife Regional Council, Fife House,
North Street, Glenrothes, Fife. KY7 5LT.
Telephone: (01592) 414141 Ext. 6337